Fabric Matching for Quilters

You're ready to make a quilt. You've chosen the pattern, settled on a size and know where it will be used.

For some quilters, the next step is the most fun—buying fabric! They charge into their local quilt shop and stack up bolt after beautiful bolt in just minutes. They seem to have an intuitive sense of the fabrics that will work in their planned design and that will blend together. Their quilts are the envy of all their friends.

For other quilters, that buying trip takes a bit longer. They deliberate over a special print and then carefully select other fabrics to coordinate. Bolt after bolt is rejected because the fabrics don't quite match the colors in the main print. But, they do finally succeed in selecting a collection of fabrics that they will like in their quilt pattern.

And then, there are those quilters who dread trying to choose fabrics. Whether it's their first

quilt or their 10th, they're nervous about making the trip to the quilt shop. They know there will be plenty of fabrics that they'll just love, but can they be put together into a quilt? Will they be boring or too busy? Will there be good contrast and a bit of spark? Will the quilt pattern stand out or disappear into the prints? Will the quilt be beautiful?

As with all things, practice makes any task easier. It is also helpful to understand how fabrics work in your quilts. In this book you will read about the characteristics of fabrics and how to apply this information to those that you will use in a quilt. You'll also learn how color influences the success of your fabric choices. Photos of many beautiful quilts and fabrics are sprinkled throughout these pages to show you that this information actually can be applied to your own quiltmaking.

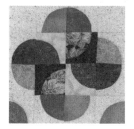

Remember, this basic information is given not to tell you which fabrics may or may not be used together, but rather to help you visualize the effect of using different types of fabrics in one quilt. I'm sure you will often think, "Hey, I already know that!" as you read through this book. I hope that the rest will help you to become more confident with your fabric choices with every new quilt you make so that you too can boldly walk into your local quilt shop and give yourself over to the pleasure of those exciting prints and colors.

Contents

Meet the Designer
Sue Harvey

Sue Harvey is freelance senior editor of *Quilter's World* magazine. She works closely with editor Sandra Hatch in planning the magazine, and editing articles and project instructions.

A native of Maine, Sue attended Husson College in Bangor, then worked for 13 years in hospital finance. She has been involved with a variety of crafts ranging from basket making to folk-art painting for more than 15 years. When she took her first quilting class in 1989, she put away all other supplies and has been designing and making quilts ever since.

Sue has designed and authored several quilting project books, including HWB's Flowers of the States and Quilting Color Magic. She teaches weekly quilting classes in a local quilt shop and for area guilds. She also teaches quilting through the area adult education program.

Sue is an avid gardener, noting that "gardening is like quilting except you use plants and flowers instead of fabric to make beautiful patchwork." She has been a master gardener for many years and coordinates the local Master Gardener's herb garden each summer.

Sue and her husband, Clayton, live in Enfield, Maine, and have one son, Joel, and one grandson, Eben.

E-mail: Customer_Service@whitebirches.com

HOUSE of WHITE BIRCHES
PUBLISHERS SINCE 1947

Fabric Matching for Quilters is published by House of White Birches, 306 East Parr Road, Berne, IN 46711, telephone (260) 589-4000. Printed in USA. Copyright © 2005 House of White Birches.

RETAILERS: If you would like to carry this pattern book or any other House of White Birches publications, call the Wholesale Department at Annie's Attic to set up a direct account: (903) 636-4303. Also, request a complete listing of publications available from House of White Birches.

Every effort has been made to ensure that the instructions in this pattern book are complete and accurate. We cannot, however, take responsibility for human error, typographical mistakes or variations in individual work.

ISBN: 1-59217-063-3
3 4 5 6 7 8 9

STAFF
Editors: Jeanne Stauffer, Sandra L. Hatch
Associate Editor: Dianne Schmidt
Technical Artist: Connie Rand
Copy Editors: Conor Allen, Nicki Lehman

Graphic Arts Supervisor: Ronda Bechinski
Graphic Artist: Vicki Staggs
Assistant Art Director: Karen Allen
Photography: Christena Green
Photo Stylist: Tammy Nussbaum

There is an overwhelming amount of fabric available to quilters today. The array of colors, patterns and styles is amazing. Quilt shops, chain stores, department stores, catalogs and Internet sites stock thousands of bolts from which every quilter may choose. The type of fabrics used in quilts is also ever expanding. Wool, flannel, iridescent velvet, lamé, chenille, synthetic suede, silk, rayon and chintz are just a few of the specialty fabrics finding their place in quiltmaking.

For most quilters, 100 percent cotton is the fabric of choice. It can be found in two categories—solid and print. There is room for both in our quilts. Each has its own characteristics and considerations for use. Solids are by their nature easy to visualize in a quilt design. Their effect is no different than that achieved by using a color pencil or plain block of color on your computer to fill in a piece in the design. On the other hand, prints are so varied in their size, design and colors that it is much more difficult to plan for their impact in a quilt. Becoming familiar with the common terms used to describe prints will make it easier to select and combine these fabrics

Solid Fabrics

Solid fabrics are those in which a single color is equally absorbed into all parts of the fibers. They are usually saturated to the point that there is no right or wrong side. There are no fluctuations in the color such as those found in the single-color hand-dyed fabrics of Shimmering Foliage.

Shimmering Foliage

Solid fabrics do vary in color, value (light or dark) and intensity (bright or subdued) from one fabric to the next. There are hundreds of different solid fabrics in every soft pastel, every rich shade, every bright hue and every subdued tone imaginable.

Solids are often used to create a certain effect in a quilt. Black or white is commonly used as a background or to set off many solid colors. Amish and Baltimore Album quilts quickly come to mind as examples of this practice. Modern quiltmakers use this same strategy with great success. The colors in these quilts seem to shine against the neutral backgrounds.

Many quilters also combine solids and prints in their quilts. The solids are often used to place emphasis on specific pieces or as a break between prints. The Crosswinds quilt uses solid triangles to create a woven effect with the many prints.

Crosswinds

Solid fabrics can add just the touch needed in your quilt design. Consider a solid when another print, no matter how subtle, will be too much, when a certain section of the pattern should stand out from those around it, when there needs to be a break when using lots of fabrics in a quilt or when small pieces cut from a print will lose their distinction.

Print Fabrics

Multicolored, one-color, large-design, small-design, realistic, imaginary, closely spaced and widely spaced—all of these describe print fabrics. They also describe visual texture: the way a fabric looks. All patterned fabrics have visual texture. Variety in texture adds interest to a quilt, but too much variety results in that "too busy" look. To better understand how to use visual texture in your quilts, it's important to become familiar with the common terms used to describe print fabrics.

Basic Vocabulary

• *Motif.* A motif is the individual design element in a print. A pin dot, a squiggle, a tiny violet, a huge rose, an animal and a stripe are all possible motifs.

Motifs range from small to large in many different shapes.

• *Ground.* The fabric behind the motif is referred to as its ground. This is not the background fabric that you choose for your quilt. Think of a floral motif scattered on cream or a star motif on red. The cream and red would be the ground colors of these two fabrics. The ground may be solid, lightly textured or patterned. When motifs are very close together, the ground color has little impact on the appearance of the fabric. On the other hand, if the motifs are widely spaced, the ground color may appear to be the overall color of the fabric. For this reason, it is important to consider the effect that this ground color will have on the overall look of your quilt.

Ground color may have little or great impact on the look of a fabric.

The colors in a print make up its colorway.

• *Colorway.* The color palette used in a print is the colorway. It may be variations of a single color as seen in tonal prints or several different colors in one print. Almost all fabrics are manufactured in several different colorways, so the floral that you love, but not in pink and blue, may also be available in your favorite colors, yellow and purple.

• *Density.* The spacing of the motifs on a fabric indicates its density. Closely spaced motifs (or packed prints) create a lot of visual texture with little attention to the individual motifs while widely spaced motifs (or tossed prints) focus attention on the motifs themselves. When two prints of the same density are used next to each other in a quilt, the lines of definition are blurred. The prints become extensions of each other.

Prints of the same density flow into each other.

layout does not refer to the way that the motifs are spaced across a fabric. They may be evenly or unevenly spaced while still being randomly oriented. Random layouts that are closely spaced are often called allover nondirectional prints. These prints are very easy to cut into pieces without regard to motif placement in the quilt.

• *Repeat.* A repeat layout places the motifs in a regular way along the length, diagonal or width of the fabric. Plaids and stripes are obvious repeat prints. However, many other prints also have repeats similar to wallpaper. Care must be taken when using a repeat layout print to cut between the repeats evenly to align with the edges of the pieces. The green border on Swedish Chain was cut perfectly to align the yellow circles with the edge of the border strips.

Print Layouts

The way the print motifs are placed on the fabric is referred to as its layout. There are five basic types of layout.

• *Random.* An irregular orientation of motifs on a fabric is referred to as a random layout. The fabric may be cut and used in any way because the motifs face in every direction as can be seen in the navy cat print in Cat Trails. Random

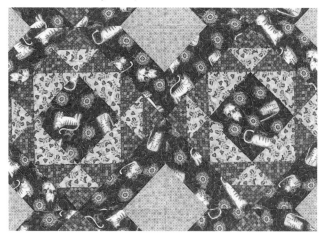

Cat Trails

Swedish Chain

• *One-Way.* In a one-way design, the motifs are placed in one direction along the length or across the width of the fabric. These fabrics require much planning to use them appropriately within a block or as elements of a quilt. When used as borders, the fabric is usually cut along its length for the sides and across its width for the top and bottom as shown in Jungle Boogie. When used in block piecing, attention must be given to the orientation of the motifs in every piece.

Cabana Fans

Jungle Boogie

between design elements or are very closely spaced. These characteristics will greatly influence the way in which these fabrics can be used.

• *Two-Way.* The motifs in a two-way design are in reverse from each other—one up and one down—along the length or across the width of the fabric. Two-way layouts offer more flexibility in cutting block and quilt pieces, especially if the motifs are small and spaced closely enough to allow more than one in a cut piece. If the motifs are very large, many of the same problems associated with one-way designs will result. In Cabana Fans, the large frond print in the outer border is a two-way design. However, the print is so close together that no special treatment was needed in cutting.

• *Scenic.* Also known as landscape prints, the design elements in scenic prints look like a painted tableau as seen in Ocean Waves. Scenics may be realistic or abstract, include a lot of ground

Ocean Waves

Pattern Scale

Scale refers to the size of the motif in a print. Many quilters gravitate toward a particular size print. In the same way that prints with the same density seem to flow into each other, so, too, do prints of the same scale appear to be similar to each other. Including prints of various scales—small, medium and large—in the quilt pieces can change this sameness.

• *Small-Scale.* Pin dots, tiny calicos, tonals, florals and checks are all considered to be small-scale prints. These prints may be random or repeating designs. Small-scale, subtle-colored prints are often used as block backgrounds instead of the more traditional solids because they tend to read as solids when used in larger pieces. However, multicolored, small-scale prints tend to read as busy. As Eight-Point Star demonstrates, a wide variety of small-scale prints form the backbone of most country-style and scrap quilts.

• *Medium-Scale.* Quilters love medium-scale prints. These are the fabrics that can easily be contained in quilt pieces. Floral Baskets uses a medium-scale print, which works as well in the basket piecing as it does in the border. The motifs

Eight-Point Star

Floral Baskets

keep their identity without overpowering the prints around them in the quilt block. There is usually no special treatment needed to use them in pieced designs. These prints can work equally well as the focus of a design or as the background for a more prominent print.

• *Large-Scale.* Large-scale prints add punch to a quilt design. Their size makes them appear closer than other fabrics in the design. These bold, graphic motifs are often showcased in block centers or in setting squares. Large-scale motifs are often fussy cut to fit in a specific-size piece—Scentimental Bouquets uses a large print as the focus of each block. They can also be randomly cut to yield a different look in each piece. Care must be taken when using these prints in small block pieces. A small portion of the print can read as a specific color or appear to be a small- or medium-scale print. These unexpected looks may upset your planned design for the block.

Scentimental Bouquets

Pattern Style

Pattern style describes the visual texture of a fabric—the motifs that make up the print. Fabric manufacturers have traditionally considered there to be only four categories of style—floral, geometric, conversational and ethnic. However,

quilters have separated many of these into other easily recognizable categories as demonstrated by the list that follows.

The style of a print does not have to be used in a certain way or in certain combinations to create a beautiful quilt. You may choose to mix several styles in one quilt or use only one. The importance of this category is that when combined with color, pattern style sets the mood of your quilt. As you read through this list of descriptions, each one is sure to bring a certain image or feeling to mind. This is the same effect that these prints give to the overall look of a quilt.

• *Floral*. (All Points Lead Home) The versatility of this print style has long been the most popular with quilters. Florals range in size from small calico flowers to huge tropical blooms. They may include only one color or many different colors.

All Points Lead Home

For this reason, they are often chosen by quilters to be the main print in a quilt. The variety makes it easy to choose a palette for the whole quilt from a single piece of fabric. Florals can also be used to create many different moods, depending on the characteristics of the print—its size, its colors, the flower(s) and the color of its ground. These fabrics can be used in bold modern designs, soft soothing designs, lively springlike designs, warm folk-art-style designs and subdued antique-looking designs. It's no wonder that these prints have been sought after for so long.

Fall Flourish

• *Nature*. (Fall Flourish) Foliage, grasses, trees, fruits, vegetables, rocks, shells and water are all images captured in nature prints. Scenic and landscape prints that include only natural elements are also included in this category. This style of print can be a realistic reproduction of the object or a more artistic rendering. These prints can be used as the main fabric in the quilt—think of a large-scale, multicolor print of autumn leaves—or as secondary, coordinating fabrics to the main print—think of a one-color print of grasses or fronds on a same-color background.

• *Stylized*. (Merry-Go-Round Medallion) Paisley, feathers, moiré, marble and trailing vines are stylized prints that stretch the limits of realistic images into more artistic versions of themselves. For example, paisley's classic teardrop shape is believed to have evolved from the stem, drooping flower head and root system of a plant. The lovely exaggerated flowers of Art-Nouveau prints, peacock feathers and fleur-de-lis are other classic examples of this category. Scrolled batiks are more contemporary examples of stylized prints.

Merry-Go-Round Medallion

• *Geometric*. (Interlocking Stars) A geometric print includes a motif that is not a picture of something in the real world. Circles and dots, squares and cubes, spirals, triangles, crescents, stars and diamonds are all examples of geometric motifs. Optical, 3-D, zigzag, chevron, basket-weave and abstract prints are also included in this category.

Interlocking Stars

Loops, wavy lines and clamshell arcs are still more examples of geometric prints. Often these motifs are used in realistic images—basket weave in a basket, stars on a flag—and in these uses are not considered a geometric. Only when used as their basic shapes are they considered part of this category of print.

• *Stripes, Plaids & Checks*. (Stars & Stepping Stones) Though actually part of the geometric style, quilters think of stripe, plaid and check fabrics to be in a category of their own. Traditionally these patterns were woven into the fabric, running along the straight and crosswise grains and at a 45-degree angle to the bias grain. This makes it relatively easy to cut these fabrics individually for use in quilt pieces. The angled look of a bias-cut is often used to add interest to borders and binding. Woven plaids, stripes and checks are most often associated with county-style quilts, but contrast nicely with florals, nature prints and conversationals to create many other moods as well. In later years, printed versions of these fabrics became popular. The lines of printed versions are not straight with fabric grain. This makes them much more difficult to cut for larger quilt pieces but their off-center look makes them a perfect choice in playful, unstructured quilt designs.

Sunshine & Shadow

Stars & Stepping Stones

• *Near-Solid.* (Sunshine & Shadows) Tone-on-tone, tonal, semi-solid, mottled—all these are common names for the near-solid print–style. These one-color fabrics tend to look like solids when viewed in a completed quilt. Most quilt designs include at least one fabric, and often many more, from this style category. Near solids are also the contemporary quilter's answer to the vibrant solids used in traditional Amish quilts. The slight nuance of texture contributed by these fabrics adds interest beyond the quilt pattern that is not reached with solids.

• *Conversational.* (Bugs & Butterflies) Prints that depict a real creature or object are included in this category of style. Conversationals are also known as novelty prints, the more familiar name to today's quilters, because the longevity of the prints is so greatly influenced by the passing

whim of popularity. Unlike the other categories of style, fabric companies seldom hold these prints from season to season. New novelty prints are produced at least every six months—usually with every season of the year. Because the motif is a real subject, conversationals are often printed as one-way designs. This characteristic makes them a challenge to use liberally in a design. Those novelties densely printed in a random layout are much easier to mass cut and use without regard to orientation of the motif.

Bugs & Butterflies

• *Ethnic.* (Star of the Orient) Fabrics made for use in another country or by a specific culture, as well as those made to replicate those of another country or culture are all included in the ethnic category. These fabrics include the Japanese indigos, African prints, South American or Mexican prints, Native American symbols, Pennsylvania Dutch motifs, and Oriental prints. Some of the fabrics actually printed in other countries may be more coarsely woven than more usual quilting fabrics, while some of these fabrics are of a very high quality.

Star of the Orient

• *Batik.* (Batik Bedspread) Mottled colors and silhouetted images cover the surface of batik fabrics. These fabrics are a subcategory of the ethnic style, but are immediately recognizable to quilters as a category of their own. Batiks

were traditionally made on the island of Java in Indonesia, where they are still a treasured art form. Most batiks used by today's quilters are made on the Indonesian island of Bali. Batiks are made by applying a wax design on the surface of a fabric piece. The fabric is then dipped or painted with ink or dye. After drying in the open air, the fabric is placed in boiling water to melt the wax. The waxed designs resist the ink or dye, leaving these areas uncolored. This process is repeated for each color in the fabric. Because the fabric has been wet, boiled and dried many times, the threads become very tight, and the fabric seldom frays or shrinks. Batik motifs fall into the same style categories as other prints—floral, nature, geometric, ethnic, novelty and near solid. They create contemporary-looking quilts when used exclusively in a design, but can also be used successfully with non-batik prints.

Batik Bedspread

• *Border Print.* (Magic Carpet Quilt) This is another print style that should be included in other categories. These wide-and-narrow-striped motif fabrics are always referred to as border prints by quilters and so are classified separately. Border prints are usually comprised of several stripes of prints that run along the fabric length. This makes them perfect for cutting long pieces to fit large quilt borders. Each stripe contains a print motif, most often stylized designs of paisleys and florals. Quilters have become very creative in the use of border prints—fussy-cut motifs are used in block piecing and in appliqué. As the demand for these fabrics has increased, fabric designers have produced border prints to coordinate with many other print styles, especially florals and novelty prints.

Magic Carpet Quilt

Putting It to Use

You are now acquainted with the two different types of fabrics—solids and prints—their characteristics, and some of the effects they have on your quilt design. This information can be easily applied to fabric selection for most quilts.

Here are a few questions to ask yourself as you stand in front of those many bolts:

1. Is there a piece in each block that I would like to emphasize? Is it small enough to benefit from the use of a solid or near solid to make it stand out among the various prints? Is it large enough to showcase a large print?

2. Are there pieces in the blocks, sashing or borders large enough to hold that one-way novelty? Will there be enough of the print to be recognized? Am I going to waste a lot of fabric cutting the spaced motifs? Would it be better to look for a novelty in a packed, random layout so I don't have to worry about direction or cutting?

3. Is there too much ground color showing in a coordinating fabric to keep it secondary to the main print? Is the ground color too strong or too light? Does it blend too much into my block background or too much into another coordinating near solid?

4. Does the main print style give the right feeling to my quilt? Is it too bold? Is it too soft to stand up to the other prints?

5. Do I have a good mix of styles? Have I chosen all florals or geometrics? Which fabrics can I substitute to add another style? Do I have a near solid or two to give good definition to my print pieces?

6. Is there good variety of scale? How many medium-scale prints are included? Is there a larger-scale fabric that I can use? Have I planned two fabrics of the same scale in adjacent pieces? Which one can be replaced? Do I have near-solid, small-, medium-, medium-large or large-scale motifs in the mix?

These questions provide answers to the type of fabrics that you may choose for your quilts. Of course, there are other factors to consider in making fabric choices—you will need to make good color choices as well. The next section will introduce color into the mix and add some hints to help you combine all this information into a successful group of fabrics for your quilt.❖

Combining Fabrics

In the same way that an artist uses paint as her means of expression, quilters use fabric. It transforms an idea into reality. It flows into all those pieces and forms a quilt. This creation may require only a few fabrics or many. In either case, the quiltmaker must be able to put together the fabric palette that will successfully translate her design into a quilt.

Add Color

Color is like magic. A design can be dynamic or subdued, just by changing the color of its pieces. Color affects the way you and others feel about your quilt. Putting colors together with fabric can be both exciting and frustrating. When dealing with a fabric of more than one color, what other colors and fabrics should you use? It is important to understand a few color theories before trying to answer that question. The following information will give you a working knowledge of the many ways that color can be used in your quilts.

The Color Wheel

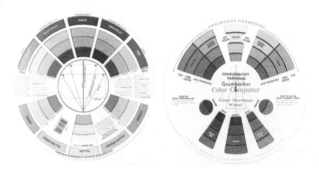

Within the circle of a color wheel are the 12 colors that form the basis for every color that you will ever choose for your quilts. If you don't already have a color wheel in your collection of quilting tools, look for one that gives you an explanation for using colors in different combinations (harmonies) and includes at least the following four variations of each color:
• Key colors—the purest form of the color—the bright, crayon-box colors.

• Tints—the pure color plus white—the lighter or pastel versions.

• Tones—the pure color plus gray—the duller or muddier versions.

• Shades—the pure color plus black—the darker versions.

The color wheel is made of two movable circles. This allows you to select a color and, through the use of blocked sections or arrows, to locate those colors that can be combined successfully. For example, you want to make a quilt with a lot of purple. By turning to violet on the color wheel, you will be pointed to the combinations of colors that will work with it—several colors that will blend (blue through red), one that will provide contrast (yellow) and two (yellow-green and yellow-orange) or three (orange, blue and yellow) that will make an exciting combination.

Fabric companies base many of their designs on the familiar color harmonies found on the color wheel. By choosing a multicolor fabric, you will be safe selecting other colors from that print to use as coordinates. By using the color wheel, you'll be safe making color combinations of your own.

Temperature

Use color to help set the temperature of your quilt. The cool side of the color wheel—blues, greens and violets—will give your quilt a calm or refreshing feeling. The warm side of the wheel—reds, oranges and yellows—will fill your quilt with heat and excitement. It is perfectly acceptable

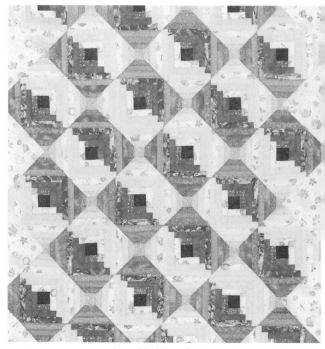

Lopsided Log Cabin

to use only cool colors or only warm colors in a quilt. Perhaps you want a quilt for your summer cottage that will have a cooling effect during warm weather or a hot quilt to bring life to a stark white room.

Most quilts, however, benefit from a combination of warm and cool colors. These quilts will have sparkle and motion that a one-temperature quilt doesn't. The warm and cool colors act in different ways—the warm colors jump out at you while the cool colors draw away. Use a warm color temperature as a way to put emphasis on certain pieces or parts of your quilt. But go easy—warm colors are powerful and can dominate your quilt, perhaps in ways that you don't want. Use them in small doses and fill the larger areas of your quilt with cooler colors. The large area of blue in the center of Galaxy cools the more vivid coral frame.

By the Seashore

Galaxy

Darker values are more dominant than lighter values. They draw away from the eye, giving the illusion of depth to a design. Lighter values seem to push out of the quilt design when used in combination with darker values. Medium values can be used to create a bridge between or to soften the effect of the more extreme darks and lights. For example, if you have decided to add a checkerboard border to your quilt but you don't want it to be the dominant design element, use either dark or light with medium in the piecing instead of dark and light together.

Value

It is more often the values of a quilt's colors, not the colors themselves, that create the design. Value describes the lightness or darkness of a color. The placement of each value in a block will determine the pieces that will stand out, recede or become neutral. Value placement is also used to create depth, dimension and motion. Rainbow of Tumbling Blocks uses three values of each color to give the appearance of cubic dimension.

Rainbow of Tumbling Blocks

Value is the key element of one-color quilts. Certainly print scale plays a part in creating the design of a one-color quilt, but it is the value of the colors that is the more distinguishing feature. Quilts made with only solids or near solids depend only on value to set off their design as demonstrated in Singing the Blues.

Singing the Blues

The value of multicolor prints must also be correctly placed in a quilt design. Remember, value is the degree of light and dark—not the color. Determining the value of multicolor prints, in relation to the other fabrics in the quilt, can be the most difficult part of making a choice. The secret is to look at all of them in black and white. This removes the color and leaves only light and dark. Line up your fabric possibilities. Squint until your eyes are almost closed to shut out color. Stand away from the fabrics before squinting to get a larger view of the whole group—you should be able to get an overall feeling of either dark or light for each fabric in comparison to another.

If a print has large areas of light and dark, be sure to evaluate how it will be cut up into your quilt pieces. If it is used in small pieces, many may look only light or only dark regardless of the value of the entire fabric piece. You'll need to go a step further than the squint test to determine its suitability.

Make a viewing template of the block piece(s) in which the print will be used. Trace or draw the piece in its exact size (no seam allowances) on a piece of paper or card stock. Cut out the shape leaving the paper around it intact. Place the open area on different sections of the print. Apply the squint test to each section with your other planned fabrics to be sure that the print will yield the correct value each time it is cut. Prepare a template for each different shape that will be cut from the multicolor print.

Intensity

Intensity is the saturation of a color. Is the color Kelly green or is it sage? Is it loud or is it quiet? Intensity is not light or dark; it is bright or dull. The key colors (or pure colors) on the color wheel are more intense than the tones (the grayed colors).

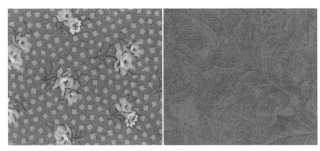

The swatch on the right has more intensity than the swatch on the left.

Think of bright red and its tone, brick red. They're the same value (squint at them to be sure), but the bright red is far more intense. Notice that the brighter color stands out from the less intense color. This can be put to good use in your quilt design by placing a more intense color in those pieces that you wish to emphasize in much the same way that you can use warm colors or different values. This strategy was used in Traveling Star Beams to make the star points seem to jump out of the quilt.

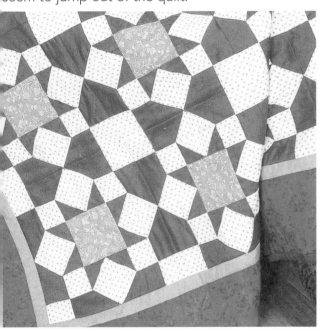

Traveling Star Beams

Think Contrast

Contrast in quilts is the difference between colors, values, scales, densities, styles, mood, layout or intensity—in other words, all the characteristics of color and fabric that you have already become familiar with. It is essential to make interesting and exciting quilt designs. Contrast occurs in two basic ways—through color and texture differences between fabrics and through color and texture differences in a single fabric.

Fabrics that are similar in value and texture (low contrast) are often used in the areas of designs in which you want the shapes to blend together or in areas that should not draw attention. This is often used in the background areas of a quilt to allow fabrics to do just as you intend—fade into the background. High-contrast fabrics are used to define the pattern of the design—they always add drama. This contrast can be achieved by using the tricks you've already learned: warm versus cool colors, low- versus high-intensity fabrics, large- versus small-scale prints and dark versus light values.

Applying these tricks to create contrast between different fabrics is pretty straightforward—use red to draw attention to certain block pieces by using cooler fabrics around it, use a darker value to set off lighter-value fabrics in the design or separate two packed prints by a near solid. But, how is contrast within a single fabric handled?

Contrast in Color

As the name implies, multicolor prints always include contrast in color. Often these contrasts are the result of the fabric manufacturer's use of color-wheel harmonies, but they must still be considered in your fabric selection. If your multicolor print includes soft and bold colors, using it as the basis for your fabric palette should result in good color contrast. However, if the print includes only soft, subdued, or bold and bright colors, you'll need to reach beyond exact color

Stars & Stripes

matches to ensure that the quilt will be neither boring nor chaotic. Add a tint or shade of a color or two in the soft, subdued print to add an accent or sparkle to the quilt. These additions do not have to be startlingly different, just a bit less grayed than the tones in the print. Add extra neutral background around the bold-and-bright colors to control their energy and provide a resting place for the eye as it travels over the quilt surface.

Cabins of the Bear

Contrast in Value

Value is essential in determining the design of a quilt. It is also essential to create contrast. Contrast in value is present in all fabrics except solids. A near-solid or tonal print has at least two values; a multicolor print may have only two or three or many different values. They may have a dark ground with light and medium motifs and medium and light accents, or a light ground with light and dark motifs and accents. The ground may also be mottled in three values and the motifs made of several light, medium and dark values.

For these reasons, it is difficult to pin down the value that a varied print will add to your quilt. If the multicolor print is to be the main print in your quilt, its block pieces are often large enough to give the same effect from the print in each piece. All God's Creatures is a good example of a large print used in both the border and in several pieces in each block. If the print will be cut into small pieces and your design depends on the contrast in value between these and other pieces, refer to Value to use a viewing template to be sure that the print yields the desired value each time it's cut.

All God's Creatures

Contrast in Intensity

Intensity differences are often present in the same print giving that bright versus dull contrast. Intensity contrast can be found in one-color prints as well as multicolor prints. The size of the high-intensity motifs and their relation to other motifs n the print will have an effect on the intensity the print will add to your quilt as a whole. The bright blue houses in the border of Autumn Apples is more intense than any other color in this quilt. Even the warm colors are tones so the more pure color of blue draws your eye around the quilt.

Autumn Apples

Imagine an all-blue fabric with a soft gray-blue background and a widely spaced bright blue vine. The relatively small amount of the bright blue motif is probably not enough to enliven a whole palette of grayed fabrics.

Now think about a multicolor print with large scattered red-violet flowers and small closely packed mauve and lavender flowers on a moss green ground. The intense red-violet in this print may be enough spark for the whole quilt without the addition of another high-intensity fabric.

Contrast in Temperature

In the same way that a spark of intensity can be achieved with one color from a print fabric, so too can the need for excitement in your quilt be satisfied by just the warm colors in a multicolor print. Again, the size of the warm motifs and the amount of the warm color in comparison to the cooler colors in the print need to be evaluated. If the warm motifs are small and widely scattered, it may be too dispersed when cut into the block pieces to have any affect on the overall temperature of the quilt. In this case, a near solid in the same warm color or another different-scale print that includes the same warm color can be used in some of the block pieces to place the color more consistently throughout the design. In Winter Wedding, the quiltmaker chose to draw on the small touches of gold in the batik print to add warmth to this otherwise icy quilt.

Winter Wedding

Contrast in Scale

Scale is especially important in one-color quilts and in blocks with many pieces. Differences in values and the size of the prints help to distinguish the design. Many small-scale or medium-scale prints used side by side create a busy, distracting look, while many large-scale prints can make the individual block pieces look like one large piece. For these reasons, it's important to vary the scale of the prints used within your blocks. This rule also applies to sashing and borders. Separate same-scale prints from each other by using another print with both a different-size motif and a different density of print.

Use a transitional fabric when shifting from one extreme in scale to another. For example, if you're using an oversize print in your block piecing, be sure to introduce a medium-scale print into the piecing in addition to small-scale prints. This creates a more natural bridge from size to size and avoids the perception that the large print is the only design element in your block. Notice the step down in scale in the blocks of Rose Garden—the large rose print in the block center to the medium-scale pink print to the small-scale burgundy print to the mottled near-solid print.

A good rule of thumb for beginners is to use large-scale prints in only medium and large block pieces. This helps to control the large print's effect on scale. When used in smaller block pieces, depending on which area of a print is cut, it may appear to be near solid or solid or medium or small in scale. Be sure to use a viewing template(s) as described in Value on different sections of your large-scale print to see how it will appear in the actual-size pieces. If it does not provide the contrast in scale that you are expecting, either

Rose Garden

change its use to larger pieces in the block, or look for another large-scale print.

Contrast in Style

Just as same-value, same-density, same-scale quilts lack excitement, using only same-style prints in a quilt can be boring. As with every rule, there are certainly exceptions. All florals look beautiful in value- and scale-based watercolor quilts. Batik quilts are striking due to their many variations in color, value and even print style. Many times same-style fabrics are used with a neutral to create lovely scrap quilts. But, generally it is preferable to vary the styles of prints to create contrast.

Combining styles can be as simple as looking for common colors in different prints. Not all colors have to be included in all the prints. A floral, geometric and stylized batik all have plum, celery and carnation in their motifs. Each also includes at least two other colors not shared by the other prints. Because the three common colors will be used in larger proportions in the quilt design merely by including each of the fabrics, the remaining colors will become secondary.

Next, think about the shapes of the motifs in the styles. Flowing edges and angular lines work well in contrast to each other as beautifully demonstrated in Star Flowers. Florals and stripes, feathers and plaids, leaves and basket weave—the different shapes of each style create contrast between the fabrics in much the same way as differences in scale draw a distinct line between pieces.

Be careful to consider the mood of the prints. The feel of the different styles should complement each other. A child's wheelbarrow in a novelty print will not work with an elegant floral even though each would be considered to have a garden theme. The styles are too different in mood. The many fabrics of Wild Safari World work together to contribute to the quilt's jungle theme.

Wild Safari World

Let's Find Fabrics

It's time! You've learned about the types and characteristics of fabrics. You've discovered how color affects the quilt design. You know that the secret to great quilts is contrast. Now, you're ready to begin choosing fabrics for your next quilt design. Give yourself a few hours, grab your color wheel and viewing template(s) and set off to your local quilt shop. Your mission? To find that one perfect lead print, several supporting fabrics, a background fabric or two and that all-important accent.

Star Flowers

Focus Fabric

This is your chance to have fun. Find that multicolor print that you just can't live without and use it for your focus fabric—the main fabric that will appear throughout your quilt design. Look for a print that has many different values to give you the greatest flexibility in adding lights and darks. Choose a medium/large- to large-scale print to create better contrast with medium- and small-scale prints. Be aware of the size of your block pieces to avoid a print that is too large to retain its identity in small pieces.

Use your viewing template(s). Don't choose a fabric that will be impossible to use in your block piecing and decide to just use it as a wide border instead. This is the fabric that you're building your whole quilt around—it should be used in all its parts. The Newcastle quilt uses a blue floral fabric in the block piecing and the borders.

Take your time making a decision—this fabric will set the mood for your whole quilt. Be sure you love not only the colors but also the feel of the print. Is it frilly? Is it country? Is it Victorian? Is it ethnic? Is it abstract? Is it frivolous? Is it childish? Make sure your focus fabric will match your image of the way your quilt will look.

Newcastle

Supporters

Now, you'll select the fabrics that will enhance your focus print. Look to your main fabric for color hints. Which colors do you like in the print? Are there any that you don't like? It isn't necessary to include every color in the print in other pieces in the quilt. But, to begin selecting fabrics, it is easier to look at fabrics in all the colors and then make a decision about those to keep and those to eliminate. You may be surprised to find that those you really didn't like in the beginning are the ones that add excitement to your palette.

First, take your main print on a tour of fabric bolts. Look at other prints in medium and small scales, remembering that these fabrics do not have to include all the same colors as your main print, only some of them. Look at other styles of prints—geometrics, florals, nature, stylized, plaids, stripes and checks, etc. And finally, look for near solids and tonals. Do not begin your search by heading straight to the near solids. Because their color and value is so obvious, near solids are almost too easy to match to a print. Many quilters begin with this style of fabric and never get away from it, so their quilts become a main print with lots of low-texture tonals around it.

Pull the bolts that exactly match your focus fabric—the easy part. Also, pull bolts in values that are lighter and darker than those exact matches. Pull bolts that vary in intensity from the colors in your main print. If your print includes all toned colors, add fabric in a more pure version of a color or two. Pull at least one bolt of a significantly darker or lighter fabric. If you are working with soft colors, this doesn't have to be deep burgundy or navy, just a darker value that will stand out among all the others that you have chosen. The same holds true for a palette of mainly dark values—choose an obviously lighter fabric than the rest. This contrast will add drama to a light palette and glow to a dark palette.

Arrange your focus fabric with all its supporters gathered round. You should have many more fabrics than you'll need at this point. Stand back and take a look at the whole collection. Do you have lots of different values? Do you have several fabrics in the same color? Is it your choice for the predominant color? Do you have only one fabric of a color? Is it an exact match? Can you find a lighter or darker value? Do you have at least one

Focus fabric and lots of possible supporters.

fabric for every color in the lead print? Are there several fabrics of the same style? Is there a good mix of scale and density?

Your answers to these questions are important. Perhaps you gravitated toward a single color because it's your favorite or because the shop has many bolts of it. Perhaps you avoided a certain color? Perhaps you chose a lot of medium values—a common trait of quilters because medium is so easy going it doesn't stand out in the crowd. Perhaps you chose lots

of florals or geometrics because they match your house décor?

Carefully consider any "offending" fabrics in relation to the other fabrics. Begin eliminating the extra fabrics in a color, value, density or style. You don't need to strive toward the same number of every fabric, but there shouldn't be glaring differences—eight blues, three greens, two pinks. In this example, try to reduce the number of blues to no more than five. Look for other fabrics to fill in the holes in your grouping. You should still have many more fabrics than you'll need. The idea is to have enough to allow you to make good decisions about the final few.

Rearrange the fabrics around your focus fabric. Try placing only the exact color matches with the focus fabric. Include different styles and densities in the group but no value or intensity changes. Does it look a little choppy or haphazard? Do the different colors seem to push against each other? Does it look bland, lacking in excitement? This is often the case when fabrics are chosen in this way. There are too many different colors whose

Focus fabric and supporters with extras removed.

Focus fabric and with exact color matches.

only relationship is the focus fabric. The only contrast may be that within the main print. The arrangement may look OK and would make a nice quilt, but it won't make a great quilt—it will lack pep and visual contrast.

Remove the exact matches and replace them with the remaining fabrics. How do they look with the focus fabric? Do any seem totally unrelated to the others and the main print without the exact match? If so, remove them. Now do they seem more exciting than the previous arrangement of exact matches? Could the selection work without adding any of the exact matches? You may find that the answer to this last question is "Yes!" Your focus fabric may have enough of each of the exact colors so it isn't necessary to repeat it with another fabric. The supporting fabrics should

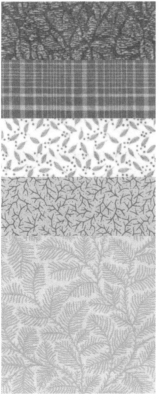

Focus fabric and supporters with exact matches removed.

complement or build on the colors and feel of your lead print—not dominate it or replace it.

Add one of the exact color matches back into the mix. If it does nothing to enliven or bring the other fabrics together, remove it and try another. There will be one or two that you will want to keep in your grouping. There may be a color with very little presence in the focus fabric or another that you want to emphasize. These colors often benefit from a fabric that is an exact match. For the other colors, different values and intensities will be enough.

Background

Next, you'll need to choose the backdrop for your block and quilt design. This area is commonly referred to as the background, while the design elements meant to stand out are called the foreground.

Traditionally, a light, neutral background is used to unite the darker and more colorful fabrics. Think of a Sawtooth Star block—the star points and center are pieced with prints in different colors while the corner squares and triangles between the points use a solid, near-solid or low-contrast print to fill in behind the star.

Most quilters today use near-solid or small-scale prints for backgrounds. It is also very common to use more than one fabric as can be seen in Memory Lane—all in the same color and the same value. These new methods add visual interest to the background areas without competing with the design fabrics in the quilt.

Look at the ground of your focus fabric for hints on background color. If it is a light background, you may want to use a background of the same

Memory Lane

Select several background-color possibilities and preview them with your focus and supporting fabrics. You'll notice that different neutral colors react differently with different fabrics in your palette. Pastel tints are deadened by cream or beige backgrounds. But cream or beige enhances the earthy, warm feeling in a quilt of autumn colors. Find the color that enhances the overall feel and colors of your quilt. When satisfied, choose more than one fabric in that color that you can use interchangeably for the background.

Background possibilities

color and value to make the ground look like it is part of the background. This will make the print of your focus fabric stand out away from the ground. If the ground has a small print or texture in it, you don't have to match it exactly. Choose two or three different textured fabrics in the same color and value. For example, if the ground is a textured pale green, use several other pale greens (toned versions are fine) with the same value.

You may like the more traditional look and use white, cream, beige or gray as your background color. It is still possible to use several fabrics in one of these colors, instead of settling for just one. These fabrics can be very close in texture and color and will appear to be the same fabric at a distance, but up close, you'll have created a bit of extra contrast.

A Zinger

This is the time to dig out your color wheel. You're looking for a color to add a bit of sparkle, a bit of zing to your quilt. It should be used sparingly and in small pieces so that it is just an accent, not a supporting fabric. A Walk Through the Garden uses small yellow squares to add a little zing to its green and purple palette.

A Walk Through the Garden

How you find the zinger fabric depends on the fabric palette that you've already put together. Is there one color that stands out or plays a bigger role in the focus fabric? If this is the case, the easiest way to select a zinger is to use a bit of its opposite (its complement) on the color wheel. For example, your main print is heavy on purple, and you've selected several purple supporting fabrics as well. Add a bit of yellow for instant sparkle.

This doesn't have to be crayon-box yellow. It could be flaxen yellow if many of your fabrics are dark—the softer color will add small spots of light in your quilt. Or it could be a rich golden yellow if many of your fabrics are subdued—the more intense color will draw the eye over the surface of the quilt.

If your focus fabric is more balanced in its colors, then you'll have to decide on a zinger color by using what you have learned about the way different colors work. First evaluate the overall look of your fabric grouping. Is it mainly pastel, tint colors; subdued, tone colors; bright, intense colors; or darker, shade colors? Does it include more cool colors or lots of warm colors?

Applying the basics about color, you know that adding a bit of a warm color to a cool quilt adds excitement. This could be your zinger. On the other hand, adding a bit of a cool color to a warm quilt adds a welcome resting spot for the eye. This could be your accent. Darker values are more dominant than lighter values. Intense colors are more dominant than low-intensity colors. Adding a much darker value to the pastel palette or a more intense color to a subdued palette will immediately draw attention to those pieces. These could be your zinger. A much lighter value added to the darker palette will seem to glow in the pieces scattered around the quilt. This could be your accent.

As you've done with the supporting and background fabrics, choose several different fabrics that you think might work as a zinger. Preview each of them separately with the rest of your fabrics. Look for the one that best gives you one of the effects described above. This will be your zinger.

Before any decision can be made about choosing your final fabrics, determine the number of fabrics that you need for your quilt design. Be sure to include your focus fabric, lighter- or darker-value fabric and zinger in your block piecing.

Then consider how many dark-, medium- and light-value fabrics you will need. Is there an opportunity in your design to substitute one fabric for another fabric in the same block or from block to block? For example, you need a medium-value mauve in certain pieces in each block. Could you substitute a medium-value rose in some of the pieces in a single block or in all of the same pieces in another block? Would this substitution work without changing the design of your block? This is a good way to use more fabrics in the overall quilt while staying with the same color theme. This also provides a larger palette to add visual texture to your piecing without competing with your design elements.

With the total number of fabrics decided, begin to eliminate fabrics from your collection, if necessary. Be sure to leave a good mix of value, scale, density and style. And be careful not to leave just one fabric of each color. Remember that choppy, haphazard look created by the exact color matches when you chose your supporting fabrics? The same thing will happen even though the fabrics may be of different values. If you have so many different colors chosen that there is only room for one fabric of each color, it is better to eliminate a color altogether and leave an extra fabric of another color.

When you've made your final selections, stand back and look at them as a whole. This will give you a better idea of how they will look together

The zinger

Choose the Final Few

By now you have a large group of fabrics from which you'll make your final selections. The good thing to keep in mind is that, if you have chosen well through all the steps that have come before, there can be no wrong choices from here. Each of the fabrics could be used in one quilt design.

Final fabric palette.

in a quilt. Is the effect pleasing to you? Is your predominant color strong enough? Is your focus fabric still the focus?

If you look at your fabric palette and love everything you see about it—buy your fabrics in the amounts you need to make your quilt. If you're still having trouble deciding on a fabric or two, buy the others in the amounts you need for your quilt. Purchase only a small piece of the troubling fabrics and the last fabric or two that you eliminated. Try them at home in a sample block to see if they actually do work in the design. Choose the ones that are most pleasing to you. Then head back to the fabric store and purchase the amounts of these fabrics that you'll need. It's far better to take a little extra time in the beginning and get those fabrics just right than to have them ruin your enjoyment of your finished quilt.

You've done it! You've taken the time to learn the characteristics of fabrics, become familiar with basic color theory and discovered the effect that contrast has on a quilt design—all to help you choose fabrics for a quilt that you'll love. Each time you go through this process, you'll find it becomes easier and easier to visualize how your fabrics will look when combined. Of course, if you're like other quilters, just as it begins to get easier, you'll decide to experiment with another style of quilt or your taste in fabrics will change. That's the beauty of quiltmaking—there is always something new to entice us into broadening our skills and our perceptions of beauty as we move from one quilt to the next. ❖

Resources

Barnes, Christine. *Color: The Quilter's Guide.*
Bothell, Wash.: That Patchwork Place Inc., 1997.

Beyer, Jinny. *Jinny Beyer's Color Confidence for Quilters.* Gualala, Calif.: The Quilt Digest Press, 1992.

Meller, Susan and Elffers, Joost. *Textiles Designs.* New York, N.Y.: Harry N. Abrams Inc., 1991.

Penders, Mary Coyne. *Color and Cloth.* San Francisco, Calif.: The Quilt Digest Press, 1989.

Alphabetical Listing of Quilts

- All God's Creatures Sampler by Connie Rand, *365 Fun-to-Stitch Quilt Blocks.*

- All Points Lead Home by Sandra L. Hatch, *Quilting to Go.*

- Autumn Apples by Christine A. Schultz, *Quick Creative Quilting.*

- A Walk Through the Garden by Jean Wells, *Quilter's World*, April 2003.

- Batik Bedspread by Connie Kauffman, *Creative Log Cabin Quilting.*

- Bugs & Butterflies by Lucy A. Fazely & Michael L. Burns, *Quilter's World*, Aug. 2003.

- By the Seashore by Holly Daniels, *Fat Quarter Quilts.*

- Cabana Fans by Linda Miller, *Quilter's World*, Aug. 2004.

- Cabins of the Bear by Julie Weaver, *Creative Log Cabin Quilting.*

- Cat Trails by Sue Harvey, *Quilter's World*, Feb. 2004.

- Crosswinds by Ruth M. Swasey, *Quick & Easy Scrap Quilting in Mix and Match Sets.*

- Eight-Point Star by Christine A. Schultz, *Quilting to Go.*

- Fall Flourish by Connie Kauffman, *Quilting to Go.*

- Floral Baskets by Kathy Reinhard, *Quilter's World*, Oct. 2004.

- Galaxy by Dorothy Milligan, *Quilter's World*, Aug. 2003.

- Interlocking Stars by Ruth Swasey, *Quilter's World*, June 2003.

- Jungle Boogie by Michele Crawford, *Quilter's World*, Apr. 2003.

- Lopsided Log Cabin by Ruth Swasey, *Creative Log Cabin Quilting.*

- Magic Carpet Quilt by Christine A. Schultz, *Quilting to Go.*

- Memory Lane by Linda Denner, *Quilter's World*, Oct. 2003.

- Merry-Go-Round Medallion by Holly Daniels, *Quilting to Go.*

- Newcastle by Larissa Key, *Quilter's World*, Feb. 2003.

- Ocean Waves by Sue Harvey, *Quilter's World*, Aug. 2003.

- Rainbow of Tumbling Blocks by Jill Reber, *101 Made-to-Fit Quilts for Your Home.*

- Rose Garden by Sue Harvey, *Quick-to-Stitch Weekend Quilts & Projects.*

- Scentimental Bouquets by Rhoda Nelson, *Quilter's World*, June 2004.

- Shimmering Foliage by Frieda L. Anderson, *Creative Log Cabin Quilting.*

- Singing the Blues by Toby Lischko, *Quilter's World*, Aug. 2004.

- Star Flowers by Jodi Warner, *Illustrated Guide to English Paper Piecing.*

- Star of the Orient by Diane Weber, *Quilter's World*, Feb. 2004.

- Stars & Stepping Stones by Jodi Warner, *Illustrated Guide to Half-Square Triangles.*

- Stars & Stripes by Dorothy Milligan, *Quilter's World*, Feb. 2003.

- Sunshine & Shadows by Connie Kauffman, *Creative Log Cabin Quilting.*

- Swedish Chain by Christine Carlson, *Illustrated Guide to Scrap Miniature Magic.*

- Traveling Star Beams by Leslie Beck, *101 Made-to-Fit Quilts for Your Home.*

- Wild Safari World by Sue Harvey, *Illustrated Guide to Panel Magic.*

- Winter Wedding by Johanna Wilson, *The Ultimate Collection of Classic Quilt Blocks.*